MW00795954

# Why We Published *The 76 Most - Common Grammar Errors*

You can sometimes bluff your way through discussions on a number of topics. But you can't fake it when your language skills are below par. People who know the language will expect you to use it correctly — if you wish to continue to move up the ladder. Colleagues, clients and others you respect will be reading what you write and listening to what you say. They don't expect you to make errors that educated people avoid.

That first impression — if it's a bad one — can prevent people from buying from you, respecting you and taking what you have to say seriously.

Frank Grazian, who has edited *communication briefings* for 13 years, brings together a variety of suggestions to help you succeed in the world of words.

Whether you use this book to win an argument or to maintain your reputation, we think it will be useful.

The Editors, *communication briefings*

© MCMXCII Communication Publications & Resources, a division of *communication briefings*, 1101 King Street, Suite 110, Alexandria VA 22314. Printed in the United States of America.

All rights reserved. No parts of this booklet may be reproduced in any form or by any means nor may any part be stored in any database or retrieval system without written permission in advance from the publisher. ISBN 1-878604-08-2.

For single copies of this booklet, or for multiple copies at a special discount, contact *communication briefings*, 1101 King Street, Suite 110, Alexandria VA 22314, or call 703-548-3800.

*communication briefings*
1101 King Street, Suite 110, Alexandria, VA 22314
© 1992 by Communication Publications & Resources

## A Number vs. The Number

*A number* is plural; *the number* is singular. *Examples:* "*A number* of accidents *are* expected." "*The number* of accidents *has* decreased."

## Along With

Which is correct? "The boss, along with her assistant, *(was, were)* present at the meeting."

*Answer: was. Why: Along with* functions as a preposition, not a conjunction. Prepositions do not make a singular subject plural.

Other prepositions to be aware of: *as well as, in addition to* and *together with.*

## Anyone (see Indefinite Pronouns)

## Apostrophes

Should an apostrophe be used in a descriptive phrase, such as *writers guide* or *teachers request?*

According to *The Associated Press Stylebook,* "The apostrophe usually is not used if *for* or *by* — rather than *of* — would be appropriate in the longer form." *Examples:* "A guide *for* writers, a request *by* teachers."

*communication briefings*
1101 King Street, Suite 110, Alexandria, VA 22314
© 1992 by Communication Publications & Resources

The apostrophe should be used, however, in a descriptive phrase when a plural word does not end in *s:* "a children's hospital."

### As vs. Because

Avoid using *as* in place of *because. Example:* "We had a day off *as* (make it *because*) it was a holiday."

Although a few dictionaries allow the substitution, especially when a sentence begins with *as,* most editors shudder at this usage.

### As Well As (also see Along With)

Be careful of using *as well as* in the following way: "Jennifer knows computer graphics *as well as* Jack." The sentence appears to mean that Jennifer and Jack know computer graphics equally well. However, to some it could mean that they both know computer graphics or that Jennifer knows computer graphics as well as she knows Jack.

### Barely (see Hardly)

*communication briefings*
1101 King Street, Suite 110, Alexandria, VA 22314
© 1992 by Communication Publications & Resources

## Because (see As vs. Because)

## Because vs. Since

Although these words are often used inter-changeably, be aware of two exceptions:

• Never use *since* to denote a cause-effect relationship. *Example:* "The boss canceled the meeting *because* (not *since*) too many people were out of town."

• Never use *since* when it might be interpreted two ways. *Example:* "*Since* we acquired the account, we've been in the limelight." Does *since* mean "*because* we acquired the account" or "*from the time* we acquired the account"?

## Being That

Stay away from using *being that*. Use *because* instead. *Example:* "*Because* (not *Being that*) I was fired, I was unable to pay that bill."

## Can vs. May

Many authorities now allow *can* to be used for *may* even in writing. However, some grammar books still make a distinction, especially in formal

*communication briefings*
1101 King Street, Suite 110, Alexandria, VA 22314
© 1992 by Communication Publications & Resources

English. They argue that *can* should be used for "able to" and *may* for "permitted to."

*Example:* "You *can* go, but you *may* not." *Our advice:* If you prefer, you may use *can* for *may* in conversation and informal writing.

## Circumlocutions

A circumlocution is a roundabout and lengthy way of expressing something. It is wordy.
*Examples:*
- a large number of (many)
- have a need for (need)
- are of the opinion (believe)
- make application to (apply)
- arrived at a decision (decided)
- on a weekly basis (weekly)
- give consideration to (consider)
- until such time as (until)

## Clarity

Avoid placing too many words between the subject of a sentence and the main verb. *Why:* The words make it difficult for the reader to grasp the main point of a sentence.

*communication briefings*
1101 King Street, Suite 110, Alexandria, VA 22314
© 1992 by Communication Publications & Resources

Consider this example: "The *CEO* (subject), concerned that the marketing department might be taking too long to come up with a detailed plan to introduce the new product, *asked* (main verb) the marketing people to work around the clock to meet the deadline."

*Suggestion:* Divide the sentence into two sentences. Tell about the action in the first sentence and give the reason in the second one.

*Revised:* "The CEO asked the marketing people to work around the clock to meet the deadline. He was concerned that the marketing department might be taking too long to come up with a detailed plan to introduce the new product."

## Clichés

Clichés are expressions that have become stale. *Examples:* "armed to the teeth," "beyond a shadow of a doubt," "wealth of information."

Yet most of us use them at times — especially when we're in a hurry and want to communicate quickly. In fact, some writers prefer to use a few clichés because their meanings are so well-known that the expressions telegraph their messages and

*communication briefings*
1101 King Street, Suite 110, Alexandria, VA 22314
© 1992 by Communication Publications & Resources

save a reader's time.

But if you want to write copy that captures readers and rivets their attention, try to come up with fresh ways of expressing thoughts. *Some suggestions:*

• Try to rewrite a cliché using a creative approach. *Example:* Take a simile, such as "as happy as a lark," and change it to "as happy as a flea on a Great Dane's back."

• Take a common expression and twist it in some way to come up with a new meaning. *Example:* "He burns the candle at neither end."

*Caution:* When using a cliché, get it right. Don't write, "They threw the baby out with the *dishwater.*" It's *bath water.* You'll call attention to yourself as being both lazy *and* illiterate.

## Collective Nouns

Words such as *audience, committee, group* and *team* are considered collective nouns. *The problem:* Should we treat them as singular or plural?

*The best advice:* Treat them as singular in American usage when they function as units. *Example:* "The group *is* (not *are*) holding *its* (not *their*) annual meeting in June."

However, treat them as plurals when they're regarded as collections of individuals. *Example:* "The group *were* in *their* seats before the CEO arrived."

If this example bothers you, recast the sentence as follows: "Group members (or 'The employees') *were* in *their* seats before the CEO arrived."

## Commas

Most business writers overuse commas. Commas should be used primarily to indicate short pauses. If in doubt, read a sentence aloud to see if a brief pause is needed. If still in doubt, leave it out.

Some points to note:

• Don't forget to use the second comma when placing a phrase in apposition to something. *Example:* "Jane, Harry's boss, extended the deadline on his project." The comma after *boss* is required.

• Always place commas both before and after the year when giving a complete date. *Example:* "April 10, 1962, was the date of her birth." But do *not* use a comma when you write only the month and the year. *Example:* "He will stay until August 1998."

*communication briefings*
1101 King Street, Suite 110, Alexandria, VA 22314
© 1992 by Communication Publications & Resources

• Note that current journalistic style calls for eliminating the last comma in a series of short items. *Example:* "He invited Nancy, Bill and Joyce." However, you may add the final comma if you wish. Just be consistent and be sure no ambiguity will result.

• Sometimes a series demands a comma. *Example:* "When filling out the form, list your name, address, sex, and housing requirements."

## Comma Splices

We cringe when we see business writers place a comma between two sentences or independent clauses. This error, called a "comma splice," is one of the most serious errors a writer can make.

*Example:* "The boss arrived late, she blamed her tardiness on car trouble." The sentences should be separated either by a semicolon or a period. If they are separated by a semicolon, the "s" in *she* should not be capitalized.

## Compare To vs. Compare With

Many authorities prefer *compare to* when citing things that are similar and *compare with* when

*communication briefings*
1101 King Street, Suite 110, Alexandria, VA 22314
© 1992 by Communication Publications & Resources

referring to things that are different. *Examples:* "She *compared* her messy desk *to* a trash heap." "He paid $20 for a tie in one store, *compared with* $40 in another."

## Comparisons

Avoid using a superlative when comparing two things. *Example:* Don't say, "Which one of the two candidates is *best?*" Change *best* to *better.*

Also be careful of *worse* and *worst. Examples:* "He took a turn for the *worse* (not *worst*)." "He wanted the promotion in the *worst* (not *worse*) way."

## Consequently (see However)

## Contractions

To determine whether you can use a contraction in informal writing, follow this guideline by Rudolf Flesch, an authority on languages: Use only those contractions that are common in speech.

*Example:* You can use *there's* for *there is* but not *there're* for *there are.*

*Note:* Most authorities permit contractions in today's business letters.

*communication briefings*
1101 King Street, Suite 110, Alexandria, VA 22314
© 1992 by Communication Publications & Resources

## Could Of

Avoid using *could of*. It should be *could have*. *Example:* "Mary *could have* (not *could of*) made more money if she had accepted the promotion." The same prohibition applies to *would of*. The problem arises because of the contractions *could've* and *would've*.

## Dangling Modifiers

Dangling modifiers occur when an introductory phrase fails to modify the word that follows the comma.

*Example:* "To plan for retirement, investments must be made carefully."

The sentence makes it appear as if investments were planning for retirement. The sentence should read: "To plan for retirement, *you* (or *a person*) must make investments carefully."

The error often occurs when the person or persons creating the action are left out of the sentence. However, it may occur when a noun or pronoun is left out of the introductory clause.

*Example:* "When starting a job, the boss should give you an orientation."

*communication briefings*
1101 King Street, Suite 110, Alexandria, VA 22314
© 1992 by Communication Publications & Resources

It should read: "When *you* start a job, the boss should give you an orientation."

## Different From

American usage prefers *different from. Example:* "His management style is *different from* (not *different than*) Dave's."

*Exception:* When the expression is followed by a clause, *different than* is acceptable. "She used an approach that was *different than* we had experienced."

## Double Negatives

Most readers will realize that the following double negative is grammatically incorrect: "He *don't* have *no* job." However, even literate writers might miss the double negative in the next sentence:

"We *won't* be able to honor your invitation to attend the affair on May 4 *nor* even the one on July 18." Change *nor* to *or. Reason:* The word *won't* covers both *the affair on May 4* and *the one on July 18.*

*Caution:* Don't confuse this construction with *neither ... nor* (see page 21).

*communication briefings*
1101 King Street, Suite 110, Alexandria, VA 22314
© 1992 by Communication Publications & Resources

## Either ... Or (see Neither ... Nor)

## Everyone (see Indefinite Pronouns)

## Exclamation Points

One sign of a weak writer is overusing exclamation points! Use them judiciously! They are designed to express emotion or special emphasis! When overused, they lose their punch!!

## Expletive (see It)

## Former

Here's an error we see frequently, especially in news releases: "He was a former teacher." Does that mean he no longer *is* a former teacher? Change it to, "He was formerly a teacher" or "He was a teacher."

## Gerunds (see Possessives Before Gerunds)

## Hardly

Avoid using *hardly* with a negative word or

*communication briefings*
1101 King Street, Suite 110, Alexandria, VA 22314
© 1992 by Communication Publications & Resources

term in a sentence. *Example:* "He *can't hardly* write his name." Make it, "He *can hardly* write his name." The same prohibition applies to *scarcely* and *barely.*

### Have Got vs. Have Gotten

American usage permits both *have got* and *have gotten* in spoken English. In the United Kingdom, *have got* is the preferred usage.

However, both expressions can be eliminated in writing, depending on meaning. *Have got* can be changed to *have.* "We *have* five computers in the office." *Have gotten* can be changed to words such as *received, obtained* or *acquired. Example:* "We *acquired* a state-of-the-art computer."

Many people object to the use of *we've got,* which means *we have got.* Your best bet: Change it to *we have.*

### Have Went (see Verbs — Principal Parts)

We shudder when we hear anyone use *have went.* It marks the user as illiterate. The proper form is *have gone.*

*communication briefings*
1101 King Street, Suite 110, Alexandria, VA 22314
© 1992 by Communication Publications & Resources

## However (also see Comma Splices)

Some business writers run two sentences together when *however* starts the second sentence. *Example:* "Some employees said they wanted a shorter week, *however,* most were satisfied." Change the comma after *week* to a semicolon or start a new sentence with *However.*

This rule also applies to *consequently, moreover, nevertheless, then, therefore* and other adverbs of this type.

## Hyphens

Hyphens should be used to clear up ambiguity. Consider the following sentence: "Small business persons were not eligible to receive the grant." The sentence refers to *"small-business* persons," not small people who are in business.

Hyphens should also be used to join two or more words that express a single concept—when these words precede a noun or follow a form of the verb *to be. Examples:* a *well-dressed* person, a *bluish-green* ink. *Note:* Do not use hyphens after words ending in *-ly. Example:* a *highly placed* source.

*communication briefings*
1101 King Street, Suite 110, Alexandria, VA 22314
© 1992 by Communication Publications & Resources

## Idioms

An idiom is an expression that often differs from the literal meaning of its parts taken as a whole. *Caution:* Never tamper with an idiom. As Theodore Bernstein notes in *The Careful Writer,* you'll do so at your own peril, "and the peril is great."

*Example:* An editor once changed the idiom *shed light* to *show light.* He argued that light can't be "shed." While his argument appeared to make sense, he was wrong to tamper with an idiom.

*Note:* Be especially alert for prepositions that are idiomatic when following certain words and preceding others. *Examples:*

- "Tracy confided her troubles *to* Pat."
- "Pat confided *in* me."
- "Fran was impatient *at* the postponement."
- "Vivian was impatient *with* her boss."

*Caution:* Many idioms are considered clichés. See the section on clichés (page 6).

Get yourself a book on idioms. One we recommend is *A Dictionary of American Idioms,* published by Barron's Educational Series Inc.

*communication briefings*
1101 King Street, Suite 110, Alexandria, VA 22314
© 1992 by Communication Publications & Resources

**If (see Whether vs. If)**

**In Addition To (see Along With)**

### Indefinite Pronouns

Pronouns such as *anyone* and *everyone* are known as indefinite pronouns. These pronouns are singular and should be treated that way.

*The problem:* To avoid sexist writing, many people are adopting the plural usage. *Example:* "*Anyone* found cheating will have *their* (not *his* or *her*) exam papers taken."

Even though many experts permit this usage in speech, many still disapprove of it in writing — even though a number of famous writers have used it.

*Our suggestion:* Handle indefinite pronouns as you would collective nouns (see page 7). When they function as units, use the singular; when they're regarded as collections of individuals, treat them as plural. *Example:* You shouldn't write, "*Everyone* should be in *his* seat (or 'in *her* seat')." *One way to handle it:* "*Everyone* should be seated."

*communication briefings*
1101 King Street, Suite 110, Alexandria, VA 22314
© 1992 by Communication Publications & Resources

**Irregardless**

Avoid this word; authorities consider it substandard. Use *regardless.*

**It**

Be careful of using *it* in an inexplicit way. *Example:* "In the brochure *it* suggests buying the product before a price increase." *The question:* What does *it* refer to in that sentence?

*Possible rewrite:* "The brochure suggests buying the product before a price increase."

*Note: It* may be used as an expletive — a word used merely to fill out a sentence. *Example:* "*It* was a good idea to go."

**It's vs. Its**

Numerous business writers confuse these words. Here's an error from a news release: "The survey shows management falls victim to *it's* own bureaucracy."

*It's* is a contraction for "it is" or "it has." *Its* is a possessive pronoun and should have been used in the example cited above.

*communication briefings*
1101 King Street, Suite 110, Alexandria, VA 22314
© 1992 by Communication Publications & Resources

### Let's

Many people follow *let's* with the wrong pronoun. *Example:* "*Let's* you and *I* go." The sentence should read, "*Let's* you and *me* go." The sentence means, "Let us — you and me — go." *Better yet:* Omit both pronouns in this instance: "*Let's* go."

### Linking Verbs

Be careful when using the following verbs: *appear, feel, look, seem, smell, sound* and *taste.* Sometimes they function as linking verbs — verbs that link the subject to the predicate. When they do, adjectives — not adverbs — should follow them. *Examples:*

"She appeared *happy* (not *happily*)."

"He felt *bad* (not *badly*) about firing Sam."

"The food tasted *different* (not *differently*) to me."

*Note:* The verbs cited above do not always function as linking verbs. *Examples:*

"Peggy looked *nervous* to Gordon." (linking verb with adjective)

"Peggy looked *nervously* at Gordon." (non-linking verb with adverb)

*communication briefings*
1101 King Street, Suite 110, Alexandria, VA 22314
© 1992 by Communication Publications & Resources

## May (see Can vs. May)

## Misplaced Phrases

Phrases that modify nouns can be misplaced in a sentence. *Example:* "Notices on bulletin boards inform employees of their rights *throughout the building.*" *Rewrite:* "Notices on bulletin boards *throughout the building* inform employees of their rights."

## Misplaced Words

Which is preferred when a writer is trying to emphasize that a person owns one chair as opposed to more than one chair? "He *only* has one chair," or "He has *only* one chair."

*Answer:* the second one, because it modifies *one chair.*

Although experts differ on the placement of words such as *only, just, even, nearly,* etc., we agree with those who require that they be placed immediately before the word or words they modify. Misplacement of these words can cause ambiguity.

However, most experts allow these words to be

*communication briefings*
1101 King Street, Suite 110, Alexandria, VA 22314
© 1992 by Communication Publications & Resources

placed before the verb in spoken language.

## Mixed Metaphors

A metaphor is a figure of speech containing an implied comparison of two things. *Example: drowning in money.*

Avoid mixing metaphors, using two images that don't make sense together. *Example:* "When the *chips were down,* he *fought fire with fire.*"

*Note:* Many metaphors have become clichés. See the section on clichés (page 6).

## Moreover (see However)

## Neither ... Nor

Use a singular verb and a singular pronoun in the following sentence: "Neither Beth nor Jean *was* ready to begin *her* duties."

However, if the subject nearer the verb is plural, use the plural forms: "Neither Beth nor the other employees *were* ready to begin *their* duties."

The same rule applies to *either ... or.*

## Nevertheless (see However)

*communication briefings*
1101 King Street, Suite 110, Alexandria, VA 22314
© 1992 by Communication Publications & Resources

## Non Sequiturs

We find non sequiturs cropping up frequently, especially in business news releases. A non sequitur is an idea or statement having no relationship to what was just said or written.

*Example:* "Born in Atlanta, she attended Yale University."

As one editor put it, "Born in Pittsburgh, I'm getting sick and tired of non sequiturs."

## Not Only ... But Also (also see Parallelism)

Be careful when using the *not only ... but also* construction that you place the same part of speech after *but also* that appears after *not only.* *Example:* "He offered *not only* his money *but also* his time."

The following would be incorrect: "He *not only* offered his money *but also* his time." *Why:* The word *offered* appears after *not only* but not after *but also.*

*Note:* In some cases the word *also* may be eliminated. *Example:* "She *not only* completed the assignment but exceeded expectations."

*communication briefings*
1101 King Street, Suite 110, Alexandria, VA 22314
© 1992 by Communication Publications & Resources

## Noun Agreement

The following sentence is incorrect: "Employees are required to cover their *computer* when they leave." *Reason:* The employees don't share a single computer.

However, there are times when a noun should remain in the singular. Here are some examples given by Theodore Bernstein in *The Careful Writer:*

"The onlookers held their *breath.*" (a figurative usage)

"The workers earned their *living.*" (an abstraction)

Making these words plural, Bernstein says, would be an example of overrefinement.

## Parallelism

When expressing ideas that should be balanced, the words used to convey those ideas should be written in parallel form. Don't write, "My boss likes *bowling* and *to fish.*" Make it *fishing* or *"to bowl* and *to fish."*

Also, when giving a series of guidelines or suggestions, be sure the sentences are in parallel

*communication briefings*
1101 King Street, Suite 110, Alexandria, VA 22314
© 1992 by Communication Publications & Resources

form. Here's an example of how *not* to do it:
"Try these three techniques to improve writing:
- "Make your average sentence 17 words long.
- "Use words your reader will understand.
- "Avoiding paragraphs of more than six lines is advisable."
The last bulleted item should read:
- "Avoid paragraphs of more than six lines."

## Parentheses

Use parentheses sparingly; they interfere with reading ease. Sometimes, parentheses signal that a sentence is becoming too complex. When possible, rewrite the sentence without the parentheses.

## Periods vs. Semicolons

Periods signal a full stop, while semicolons indicate a shorter stop. Use periods to end sentences; use semicolons to separate closely related clauses, such as those in this sentence.

## Possessives Before Gerunds

A gerund is a verb form used as a noun; it usually ends in *-ing: walking, swimming, talking.*

*communication briefings*
1101 King Street, Suite 110, Alexandria, VA 22314
© 1992 by Communication Publications & Resources

When a noun or pronoun comes immediately before a gerund, it must be in the possessive case. *Examples:*

"*Jerry's* (not *Jerry*) borrowing money was a last-ditch effort."

"Grace disliked *his* (not *him*) talking during meetings."

*Caution:* Don't confuse gerunds with participles — verb forms that sometimes end in *-ing* but don't serve as nouns. Note the difference in the following sentences:

"Jack's *talking* annoyed others." (Here the emphasis is on the act of talking, a gerund.)

"We saw Jack *talking*." (Here the emphasis is on Jack. *Talking* is a participle, not a gerund.)

## Prepositions

Some people contend that a preposition should never be placed at the end of a sentence. They argue that in Latin the word means "stand before."

True, but English use since Chaucer has established a tradition that not only permits the use of a preposition at the end of a sentence but also encourages the construction when a preposition is

*communication briefings*
1101 King Street, Suite 110, Alexandria, VA 22314
© 1992 by Communication Publications & Resources

needed to supply a strong ending.

As an article in a prestigious English journal once noted: "A preposition is a good word to end a sentence with."

## Pronoun References

Avoid using one pronoun that can create ambiguity by referring to two things or people. *Example:* "Michael waved to Hal as he was leaving his office." Who was leaving the office: Michael or Hal?

*Suggested rewrites:*

"As Hal was leaving his office, Michael waved to him."

"As Michael was leaving his office, he waved to Hal."

## Pronunciation

We decided to include a brief section on pronunciation in this book because readers of *communication briefings* often ask us for the "correct" pronunciation of certain words.

*The problem:* Dictionaries list variant pronun-

*communication briefings*
1101 King Street, Suite 110, Alexandria, VA 22314
© 1992 by Communication Publications & Resources

ciations without indicating which pronunciation they prefer. Yet most people want something to guide them.

*Our suggestion:* Get a copy of the *NBC Handbook of Pronunciation* (see section titled "More resources for you" on page 45). Here are a few controversial words covered in the handbook:

- accelerate (ak SEL uh rayt)
- coherent (koh HEER ant)
- coupon (KOO pon)
- data (DAYT uh)
- era (EER uh)
- harassment (huh RAS ment)

Be especially careful about the pronunciation of the following words: athlete (ATH leet — not ATH uh leet), hindrance (HIN drans — not HIN der ans), nuclear (NOO klee ur — not NOO ku lar), and often (AW fuhn — not OFF ten).

## Question Marks

Never use a question mark after an indirect question. *Example:* "Faith asked Dennis what he thought of the project." Always use one after a

*communication briefings*
1101 King Street, Suite 110, Alexandria, VA 22314
© 1992 by Communication Publications & Resources

direct question. *Example:* "What do you think of the project, Dennis?"

## Quotation Marks — Part I

Confused about when to use quotation marks around words that are not part of a quotation? Here's a guideline that should help:

Use the marks around words used in a special sense (an ironical sense, for example), unfamiliar words being introduced to the reader and words being defined.

Some stylebooks allow italics for these purposes. *Our suggestion:* Be consistent. That's what counts.

## Quotation Marks — Part II

Here are some rules about where to place other punctuation marks in relation to quotation marks:

• Commas and periods fall within quotation marks. *Example:* "Hello," he said. "I've heard a lot about you."

• Colons and semicolons fall outside quotation marks. *Example:* "He defined 'serendipity'; the word came from *The Three Princes of Serendip*."

*communication briefings*
1101 King Street, Suite 110, Alexandria, VA 22314
© 1992 by Communication Publications & Resources

• Dashes, exclamation points and question marks fall within the quotation marks only when they apply to the quoted material; otherwise they fall outside.

*Example:* Tom asked, "What is the matter?"
*Example:* "Can you define 'serendipity'?"

## Redundancies

Redundancies occur when one word contains part of the idea expressed in another word or term. *Example:* "revert back." *Revert* means "to go back in action, thought, speech, etc." Therefore, the word *back* is redundant.

Redundancies do not add emphasis, as some people think; they merely serve to mark a writer as inexperienced. Here are some commonly used redundancies:

- basic fundamentals (fundamentals)
- close proximity (proximity)
- completely full (full)
- consensus of opinion (consensus)
- continue on (continue)
- cooperate together (cooperate)

*communication briefings*
1101 King Street, Suite 110, Alexandria, VA 22314
© 1992 by Communication Publications & Resources

- end result (result)
- first began (began)
- foreign imports (imports)
- future prospects (prospects)
- many in number (many)
- new innovation (innovation)
- other alternative (alternative)
- past experience (experience)
- present incumbent (incumbent)
- postpone until later (postpone)
- sufficient enough (sufficient)
- true facts (facts)

## Scarcely (see Hardly)

## Semicolon (see Periods vs. Semicolons)

## Sentence Fragments

A sentence fragment is an incomplete sentence. Usually, it omits either a subject or a predicate. *Example:* "People doing their best."

Sometimes it contains a subject and a predicate but fails to qualify as an independent clause. *Example:* "When Sally lost her temper."

*communication briefings*
1101 King Street, Suite 110, Alexandria, VA 22314
© 1992 by Communication Publications & Resources

In the following example, what appears to be the second sentence is a fragment: "Tom completed the project on time. Because his boss said he would receive a bonus if he met the deadline." The statement should be changed to read: "Tom completed the project on time, because his boss said he would receive a bonus if he met the deadline."

In most cases, you should avoid sentence fragments. However, they may be used as the answer to a question: "Where did Chris buy that word processor?" "At the local computer store."

They may also be used for emphasis. *Example:* "No questions asked!"

*Note:* Don't confuse sentence fragments with sentences that give a command. *Example:* "Learn how to handle irate customers."

### Sequence of Tenses

Which is correct? "John said the weather *is (was)* perfect for an office picnic."

Answer: *was. Why:* What John actually said was, "The weather *is* perfect for an office picnic." But when you quote him indirectly and use the word *said* — a verb in the past tense — as the

*communication briefings*
1101 King Street, Suite 110, Alexandria, VA 22314
© 1992 by Communication Publications & Resources

main verb in the sentence, you must link the subordinate verb to it in proper time sequence. Therefore *is* must be changed to *was.*

*An exception:* When the "he said" or "she said" phrase does *not* appear at the beginning of the sentence, the rule fails to apply. *Example:* "The weather, John said, *is* perfect for an office picnic."

*Another exception:* a universal truth: "Trish said the earth *is* the planet we inhabit."

## Shall vs. Will

American usage no longer makes a distinction between *shall* and *will.* Most writers use *will* in all cases. But for those who would like to review the almost-forgotten rule, here it is:

Use *shall* with the first person *(I, we)* and *will* with all other persons *(you, they, she, he, it).* When you want to express determination, reverse the order: "I don't care what you say; he *shall* attend."

*Note: Shall* is still used in polite questions: "*Shall* I pour tea?" *Also: The Associated Press Stylebook* continues to make some distinction between *shall* and *will* but allows either *shall* or

*communication briefings*
1101 King Street, Suite 110, Alexandria, VA 22314
© 1992 by Communication Publications & Resources

*will* in first-person constructions that do not emphasize determination.

## Shifts

Avoid shifts in verb tense. *Example:* "Janice tried to motivate her staff. She *gives* (make it *gave*) her people a day off, because they met their deadlines."

Also, avoid shifts in number. *Example:* "A *person* (make it *people*) must take *a number* (make it *numbers*) when *they* come in." *Note:* Some authorities now allow a number shift because of the he/she problem. We advise you to stay away from it in writing.

## Since (see Because vs. Since)

## Split Infinitives

Most authorities allow infinitives to be split, but only when the construction is needed to communicate the meaning and won't appear awkward. *Example:* "Bob wanted *to really make* a difference."

*communication briefings*
1101 King Street, Suite 110, Alexandria, VA 22314
© 1992 by Communication Publications & Resources

## Subject-Verb Agreement (also see Clarity)

Subject-verb agreement ensnares many business writers, especially in sentences where the subject is separated from the verb by several words. In a short sentence, no confusion occurs. *Example:* "Repetition *helps* us gain confidence." However, look at what often happens when the subject *(repetition)* is separated from the verb *(helps)*: "The repetition of exercises *help* us gain confidence." *Helps* is still the right word to use.

Also, watch for the contraction *here's*. *Example:* "*Here's* five ways to solve the problem." *Here's* means *Here is*. The sentence should start with *Here are*.

## Subjunctive Mood

Although some grammar experts no longer require the use of the subjunctive, we advise business writers to use it in two instances — when expressing a condition contrary to fact and when expressing a desire. *Examples:*

"If I *were* (not *was*) a better writer, I could qualify for that job." (contrary to fact)

"I wish I *were* (not *was*) a better writer." (desire)

*communication briefings*
1101 King Street, Suite 110, Alexandria, VA 22314
© 1992 by Communication Publications & Resources

## That (also see Where vs. That)

Some writers go to extremes to eliminate the word *that* in their sentences. *Our suggestion:* Be careful about omitting *that* when its omission might make a sentence unclear.

*Example:* "She said yesterday you were brilliant." That sentence could be interpreted two ways: "She said *that* yesterday you were brilliant" or "She said yesterday *that* you were brilliant."

Follow this advice from *The Associated Press Stylebook:* "When in doubt, include *that.* Omission can hurt. Inclusion never does."

## That vs. Which

Use *that* when the words following it are necessary to identify the word *that* refers to. *Example:* "The river *that* flows by my door is rising."

You can't remove the "that clause," because you wouldn't know which river is being referred to. The sentence would simply read: "The river is rising."

Use *which* when the words following it are not necessary to identify the word it refers to.

*communication briefings*
1101 King Street, Suite 110, Alexandria, VA 22314
© 1992 by Communication Publications & Resources

*Example:* "The Delaware River, *which* flows by my door, is rising."

You *can* remove the "which clause," because you would know which river is being referred to — the Delaware River. The sentence would read: "The Delaware River is rising."

*Note:* When using *which,* use commas to separate the clause. When using *that,* don't use commas.

## The Number (see A Number vs. The Number)

## Their vs. They're vs. There

Don't confuse these words. *Their* is a pronoun meaning "of or belonging to them"; *they're* is a contraction meaning "they are"; *there* is an adverb indicating place or location, or an interjection. *Examples:* "*Their* projects are finished."

"*They're* going to the meeting." "*There* is a long line *there.*"

## Then (see However)

*communication briefings*
1101 King Street, Suite 110, Alexandria, VA 22314
© 1992 by Communication Publications & Resources

**There (see Their vs. They're vs. There)**

**Therefore (see However)**

**They're (see Their vs. They're vs. There)**

## This

Although some authorities allow *this* to refer to the whole idea of a preceding sentence, be sure that the word can carry the load.

*Example:* "The consultant tried to show us how to increase cash flow while paying our bills on time. However, *this* was not easy to carry out." Make the second sentence, "However, *this procedure* was not easy to carry out."

*Tip:* Try to find a noun that describes the action and use it with *this.*

## Together With (see Along With)

## Up and Down

Avoid adding *up* or *down* to verbs that don't need these adverbs. You'll either weaken the punch

*communication briefings*
1101 King Street, Suite 110, Alexandria, VA 22314
© 1992 by Communication Publications & Resources

of the original words or create redundancies. *Some examples:*

- condense down (condense)
- drop down (drop)
- face up (face)
- head up (head)

*Caution:* Some expressions require *up* or *down* to communicate their meaning. Removing the adverbs would change what they mean. *Examples:* back down, pick up.

*Suggestion:* Whenever you discover a required *up* or *down* after a verb, see if you can find a stronger verb, one that adds punch to your sentence. If not, however, don't force it.

*Example:* "The promotion *picked up* his confidence." Change *picked up* to *raised* or *restored,* depending on meaning.

**Use To vs. Used To**

The correct expression is *used to. Example:* "They *used to* (not *use to*) hold meetings every week."

**Verbs — Principal Parts**

Most verbs are regular; they form their past tense and past participle by adding *-d* or *-ed.*

*communication briefings*
1101 King Street, Suite 110, Alexandria, VA 22314
© 1992 by Communication Publications & Resources

*Example:* verb — *hope,* past tense — *hoped,* past participle — *have hoped* or *had hoped.* Irregular verbs, on the other hand, do not follow this simple rule. Here are some of the irregular verbs that give people the most trouble:

| Verb | Past Tense | Past Participle |
|------|------------|-----------------|
| arise | arose | arisen |
| begin | began | begun |
| bring | brought | brought |
| burst | burst | burst |
| choose | chose | chosen |
| get | got | got or gotten |
| go | went | gone |
| lay (place) | laid | laid |
| lead | led | led |
| lie (recline) | lay | lain |
| raise | raised | raised |
| rise | rose | risen |
| shrink | shrank | shrunk |
| speak | spoke | spoken |
| wring | wrung | wrung |

*communication briefings*
1101 King Street, Suite 110, Alexandria, VA 22314
© 1992 by Communication Publications & Resources

### Where vs. That

Avoid using *where* for *that*. *Example:* "I read *that* (not *where*) our company has issued new bonds."

### Whether vs. If

Most experts agree today that *whether* and *if* are interchangeable. However, a few still prefer *whether* when an alternative choice is indicated. *Example:* "Kirk expects to attend *whether* he is sick or well."

### Which (see also That vs. Which)

Some experts do not allow *which* to refer to the whole idea of a preceding clause. *Example:* "She is good at managing, *which* makes her valuable." One way to change it: "Her ability to manage well makes her valuable."

### Which vs. Who vs. That

Don't use *which* when referring to people. Use *who, whom* or *that. Example:* "The organization has 5,000 members — all of *whom* (not *which*) are

*communication briefings*
1101 King Street, Suite 110, Alexandria, VA 22314
© 1992 by Communication Publications & Resources

interested in self-improvement."

*Note: That* may be used for either people or things, but *who* and *whom* are preferred for people.

## Who vs. Whom

Determining when to use *who* and when to use *whom* gives many business writers fits. *The rule:* Use *whom* when the word serves as an object and *who* when it serves as a subject. *Examples:*

"*Whom* did they elect?" In this case *whom* is the object of the verb *elect.*

"*Who* is the best person for the job?" Here, *who* is the subject of the verb *is.*

A problem arises in complex sentences when the word serves as the subject of a dependent clause, but the clause serves as the object of the main verb.

*Example:* "He forgot who called." In this case, *who* is the subject of *called,* and the clause *who called* is the object of the verb *forgot. Another example:* "They disagreed as to *who* should be hired." *Who* serves as the subject of *should be hired,* not as the object of *to.* The clause *who should be hired* is the object of *to.*

*communication briefings*
1101 King Street, Suite 110, Alexandria, VA 22314
© 1992 by Communication Publications & Resources

*Suggestion:* You might want to rewrite a sentence to avoid the use of *whom,* because many people consider it to be stilted.

*Note:* The same rules apply to *whoever* and *whomever.*

## Whoever vs. Whomever (see Who vs. Whom)

## Who's vs. Whose

*Who's* is a contraction meaning "who is" or "who has." *Example:* "*Who's* seeking that job?" *Whose* is a pronoun or possessive pronoun adjective that means "belonging to whom" or "made or done by whom or which." *Examples:* "*Whose* is this?" "*Whose* book is lost?"

## Will (see Shall vs. Will)

## Worse vs. Worst (see Comparisons)

## Would Have

Avoid using the expression *would have* when

*communication briefings*
1101 King Street, Suite 110, Alexandria, VA 22314
© 1992 by Communication Publications & Resources

you mean *had. Example:* "If you *had* (not *would have*) completed the project on time, we would have been able to present it today."

## Would Of (see Could Of)

## You and I

Many business writers misuse *you and I. Some examples:*

"Between *you and I,* there's no problem."

"He's smart, just like *you and I.*"

Both *between* and *like* are prepositions that take an object. Words following them should be *you and me.*

Here are ways the phrase *you and I* is handled correctly:

"*You and I* are going to work together."

"I realize that *you and I* deserve the award."

In the first case, the phrase *you and I* serves as the subject of the sentence and, in the second case, it serves as the subject of the "that clause."

*Note:* Some readers might argue that *I* is the correct word following *like,* because the phrase means "smart just like *you and I* are smart." Not

*communication briefings*
1101 King Street, Suite 110, Alexandria, VA 22314
© 1992 by Communication Publications & Resources

so. *You and I* would be correct if the preposition *like* had been replaced by the conjunction *as*.

## Your vs. You're

*Your* is a pronoun meaning "of or belonging to you"; *you're* is a contraction meaning "you are." *Examples:* "*Your* lunch is ready." "*You're* fortunate."

Even business writers who know better often get sloppy with these words. Proofread carefully.

*Tip:* Use the find-and-replace function on your computer to search for *your* to make sure you haven't inadvertently used it to mean "you are."

*communication briefings*
1101 King Street, Suite 110, Alexandria, VA 22314
© 1992 by Communication Publications & Resources

## More resources for you

The following books provide valuable information on grammar and language. The editors of *communication briefings* rely on them and recommend them as desktop references.

• *American Usage & Style: The Consensus,* by Roy H. Copperud, Van Nostrand Reinhold Co., 115 5th Ave., New York, NY 10003.

• *The Associated Press Stylebook and Libel Manual,* Addison-Wesley Publishing Co., 1 Jacob Way, Reading, MA 01867.

• *The Bedford Handbook for Writers,* by Diana Hacker, St. Martin's Press Inc., 175 5th Ave., New York, NY 10010.

• *The Careful Writer,* by Theodore M. Bernstein, Atheneum Publishers, 866 3rd Ave., New York, NY 10022.

• *The Elements of Grammar,* by Margaret Shertzer, Collier Books, Macmillan Publishing Co., 866 3rd Ave., New York, NY 10022.

• *Everything You Need to Know About Grammar,* by Leo Hamalian and Frederick R. Karl, Ballantine Books, Random House Inc., 201 E. 50th St., New York, NY 10003.

*communication briefings*
1101 King Street, Suite 110, Alexandria, VA 22314
© 1992 by Communication Publications & Resources

• *Harbrace College Handbook,* by John C. Hodges and Mary E. Whitten, Harcourt Brace Jovanovich Inc., College Text Division, 7555 Caldwell Ave., Chicago, IL 60648.

• *NBC Handbook of Pronunciation,* by Eugene Ehrlich and Raymond Hand Jr., Harper Perennial, a division of HarperCollins Publishers, 10 E. 53rd St., New York, NY 10022.

• *The Wordwatcher's Guide to Good Writing & Grammar,* by Morton S. Freeman, Writer's Digest Books, 1507 Dana Ave., Cincinnati, OH 45207.

• *The World Almanac Guide to Good Word Usage,* edited by Martin Manser with Jeffrey McQuain, Avon Books, 1350 Avenue of the Americas, New York, NY 10019.

The editors also recommend:

• *The Glossary of Misused Words and Phrases,* from the editors of *communication briefings*, Communication Publications and Resources, 1101 King Street, Suite 110, Alexandria, VA 22314.

*communication briefings*
1101 King Street, Suite 110, Alexandria, VA 22314
© 1992 by Communication Publications & Resources

## Sharing *The 76 Most-Common Grammar Errors ... And How to Avoid Them*

If you agree that others in your organization should have a copy of *communication briefings' The 76 Most-Common Grammar Errors ... And How to Avoid Them,* we have a special price for you.

You can get copies of this booklet for only $6.50 each when you order six or more at any one time. That's $6.00 off the regular price of $12.50.

When you consider what *The 76 Most-Common Grammar Errors* can do for all of your employees and everything they write, this is an investment you shouldn't pass up.

Order with the form on page 48.

## Get ideas that work from *communication briefings*

Since 1981, *communication briefings* has been offering the latest on what's working to communicators and managers every month.

This highly regarded, eight-page newsletter is written for your busy schedule – to the point with no puff.

You get the basics on what you need to know and do to put ideas to work for you.

If you join the more than 50,000 colleagues and competitors who subscribe to *communication briefings,* you'll get our no-nonsense, money-back offer:

Subscribe now. If at any time during the first year of your subscription you find *communication briefings* isn't for you, cancel. Your entire $79 will be refunded. No questions asked.

Subscribe with the form on page 48.

*communication briefings*
1101 King Street, Suite 110, Alexandria, VA 22314
© 1992 by Communication Publications & Resources

## Order Form

❏ Please send me _____ copy(ies) of *The 76 Most-Common Grammar Errors* @ $12.50 (U.S.) each for a total of $_____.

❏ Please send me _____ copies of *The 76 Most-Common Grammar Errors* @ the special rate of $6.50 each (U.S.) for a total of $_____. (You must order 6 or more for the special $6.50 ea. price.)

❏ Yes, I'm subscribing to *communication briefings*. Please enter my one-year (12 issues) subscription @ $79 (U.S.) – $99 (U.S.) in Canada, $119 (U.S.) in all other countries.

❏ My payment of $_____ is enclosed.

❏ Please charge my: ___Visa ___MasterCard ___AMEX

Name on Card: _____ Exp. date: _____

Card #: _____

Signature: _____

(payment must accompany order • please type or print clearly)

Name: _____

Title: _____

Company: _____

Address: _____

City: _____ State: _____ ZIP: _____

Phone: (   ) _____ FAX: (   ) _____

**Mail to: Special Order Dept.**
*communication briefings*
**1101 King Street, Suite 110**
**Alexandria, VA 22314**

**Credit card holders can order by phone: 800-888-2086**
**(In VA, call 703-548-3800) or FAX: 703-684-2136.**

**NOTE:** Payment in U.S. funds must accompany order • Make checks payable to CP&R • Orders outside U.S. and Canada, add $3 (U.S.) for each booklet to cover additional shipping and handling costs • Add appropriate sales tax to booklets shipped to VA and DC • Prices subject to change.

*communication briefings*
1101 King Street, Suite 110, Alexandria, VA 22314
© 1992 by Communication Publications & Resources